W9-AET-869

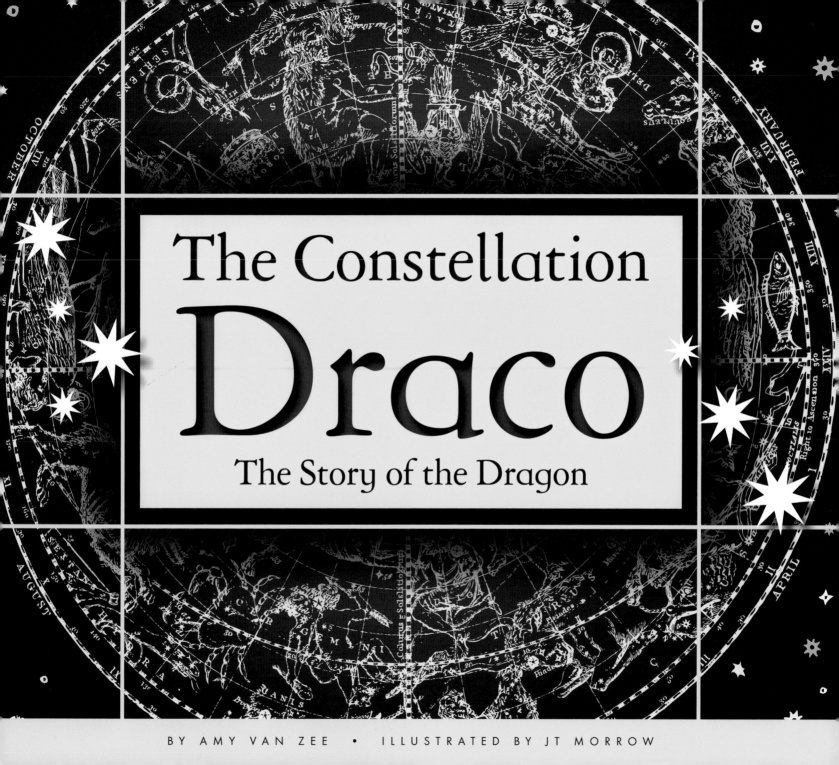

The Constellation
Draco
The Story of the Dragon

BY AMY VAN ZEE • ILLUSTRATED BY JT MORROW

The Child's World

Published by The Child's World®
1980 Lookout Drive • Mankato, MN 56003-1705
800-599-READ • www.childsworld.com

Acknowledgments
The Child's World®: Mary Berendes, Publishing Director
Red Line Editorial: Editorial direction and production
The Design Lab: Design

Photographs ©: Thinkstock, 5, 16; NASA/JPL-Caltech, 6, 7; Yganko/
Shutterstock Images, 9; X-ray: NASA/CXC/SAO; Optical: NASA/
STScI, 10; NASA, ESA, and The Hubble Heritage Team (STScI/AURA),
11; Library of Congress, 13; St. Nick/Shutterstock Images, 14; Davor
Pukljak/Shutterstock Images, 15; Hulton Archive/Getty Images, 17;
tratong/Shutterstock Images, 26; Hemera Technologies/Thinkstock, 27

Design elements: Alisafoytik/Dreamstime

ISBN: 9781623234850
LCCN: 2013931375

Printed in the United States of America
Mankato, MN
April, 2014
PA02229

ABOUT THE AUTHOR

Amy Van Zee is an editor and writer who lives near Minneapolis, Minnesota. She has an English degree from the University of Minnesota and has contributed to dozens of educational books.

ABOUT THE ILLUSTRATOR

JT Morrow has worked as a freelance illustrator for more than 20 years and has won several awards. He also works in graphic design and animation. Morrow lives just south of San Francisco, California, with his wife and daughter.

Table of Contents

CHAPTER 1

The Constellation Draco

THE STUDY OF SPACE
Astronomy is the study of stars, planets, and other objects in outer space. Today's astronomers have powerful telescopes to see faraway stars. But even in the far past, people used stars to tell time. They used stars to guide them from one place to another.

What do you see when you look at the stars? Do you see princesses and heroes? Do bulls, scorpions, or bears catch your eye? The earliest people gazed at dots of light in the black sky. They imagined lines connecting the stars. These imaginary lines formed people and creatures. These star pictures are called constellations.

The constellation Draco is known as the dragon. Its thin body twists through the sky. It lies near the **North Star**, Polaris. It is the eighth-largest constellation. Stargazers have seen Draco in the night sky for thousands of years. And for just as long, they have told stories about the mighty serpent.

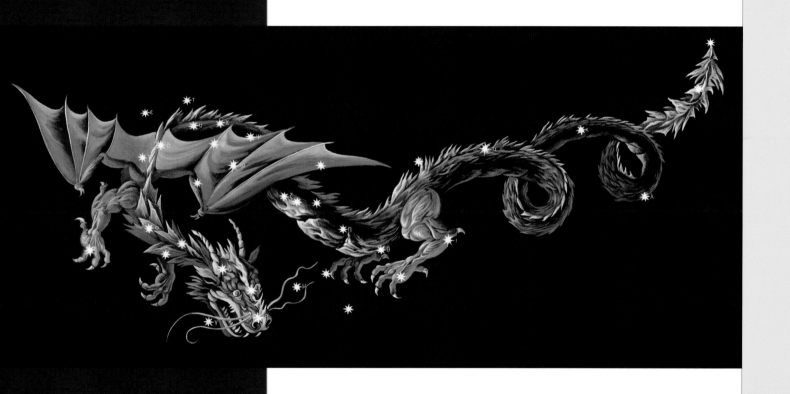

▼ *The large constellation Draco twists through the night sky.*

From Earth, most stars look like tiny points of light. But most stars are thousands of times larger than Earth. The Sun is the closest star to Earth. Its light and heat are seen and felt all over the planet. Stars come in many sizes, from dwarfs to giants. Compared to other stars, the Sun is average size. The Sun weighs 333,000 times as much as Earth. Stars also come in many colors, from red to yellow to blue. A star's color tells scientists how hot it is. Blue stars are the hottest.

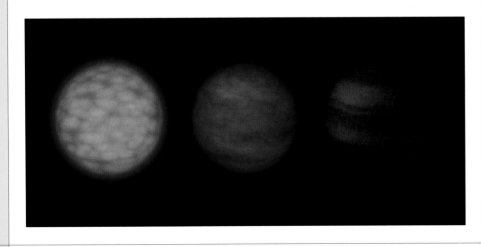

◄ Stars come in many colors

Stars are born from clouds of dust and gas in space.

Each star goes through a life cycle over billions of years. First, a cloud of dust and gas gathers. The cloud begins to spin. It starts slowly. Eventually its **gravity** pulls in more dust and gas. The cloud spins faster and faster. The core becomes very hot. Burning hot temperatures and high pressure create a burst of energy. The star is born!

Draco has 31 stars. They make up a tail, body, head, and flicking dragon tongue. Draco's head is an **asterism**. Two of the stars in the head are Rastaban and Eltanin. These are the eyes of the great dragon. Eltanin is the brightest star in the constellation. The ancient Arabs named it. Eltanin means "dragon's head." Ancient Egyptians built temples facing Eltanin.

Thuban is the best-known star in Draco. It is part of the dragon's body. It has an important history. Today, Polaris is Earth's **polestar**. This means Earth's North Pole points to it. But around 2800 BC, Thuban was Earth's polestar. How did this change? Earth rotates on its **axis**. This axis is slightly tilted. Earth's rotation is a little wobbly. Earth's wobbly rotation means the North Pole has moved slightly over thousands of years. Today it points to Polaris.

▶ *Opposite page: The stars of Draco*

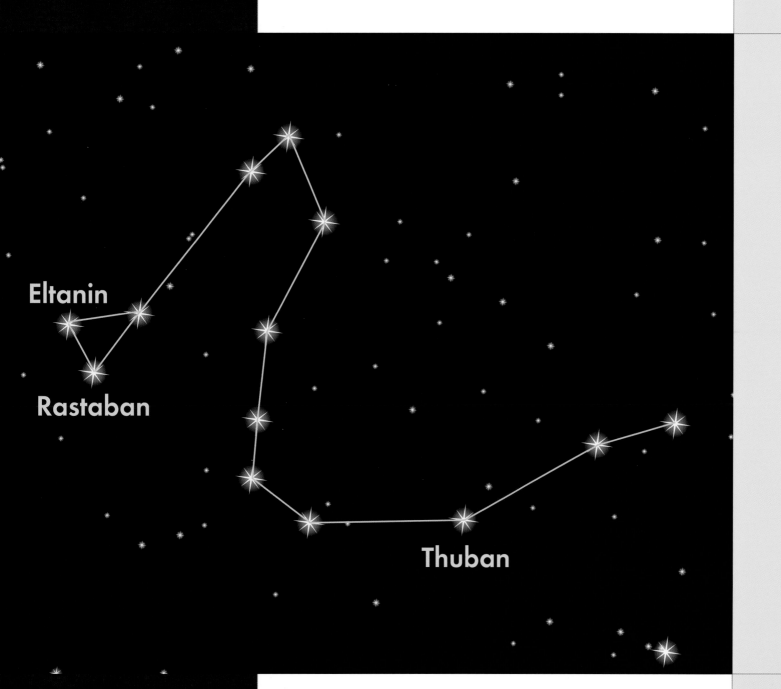

Eltanin

Rastaban

Thuban

Draco is home to more than just stars. Astronomers discovered the Cat's Eye **Nebula** in Draco in the 1700s. This nebula appears as a bright, blue-green disk through a telescope. It was created from a dying star. The star's outer layers were stripped away. The gases around the star began to glow brightly. Scientists believe this happened between 1,000 and 1,300 years ago. We still see these gases glowing today.

Draco is also home to the distant Spindle **Galaxy**, also called M102. A galaxy is a massive grouping of stars and objects. There might be billions or trillions of galaxies in the **universe**! From the front, M102 would look flat and round, like a coin.

▲ *The Cat's Eye Nebula*

But we see the galaxy from its side. So it appears long and thin from Earth.

CHAPTER 2

The Origin of the Myth of Draco

Astronomy is one of the oldest sciences. The ancient astronomer Ptolemy lived from about 100 to 200 AD. He wrote down what earlier astronomers had seen in the skies. He wrote down what he learned by watching the stars, too. He created a catalog of 48 constellations, including Draco.

But people saw Draco long before Ptolemy. The ancient people of **Mesopotamia** saw the dragon with wings. Later, the early Greeks changed the constellation. They saw the stars of Draco's wings as part of the constellation Ursa Minor. So Draco became a wingless dragon.

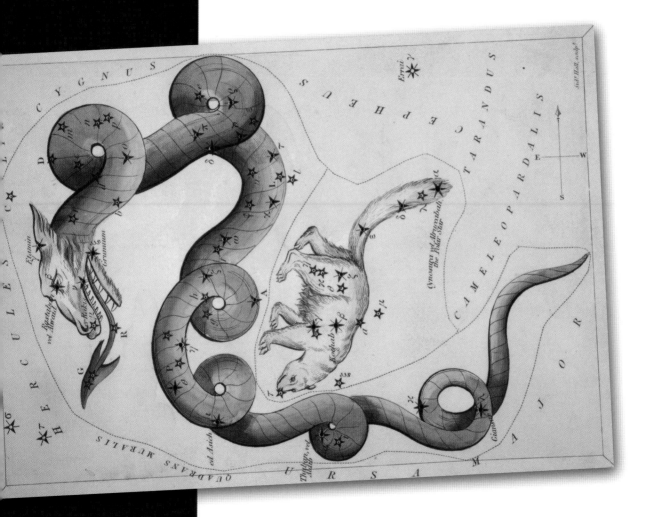

Many stories are told about Draco. But the main myths about the dragon come from Greek **mythology**. In one Greek myth, the dragon is part of an epic battle. The Greek gods fought a group of giants. The goddess Athena caught Draco and pitched it into the northern sky. There the cold air froze it in a coiled position.

The dragon is part of the story of Jason and the Argonauts. These men had to find a golden fleece, or sheep's skin. But a fierce dragon guarded the fleece. Jason got help from a sorceress. He overcame the dragon and took the fleece.

▲ Athena was the goddess of wa and wisdom.

Jason conquers the dragon and claims the fleece with the sorceress's help.

The dragon is a common character in world mythology. The stories of many cultures tell of terrifying dragons. In Greek mythology, dragons are often guarding something. Dragons are symbols of watchfulness. In northern skies, the constellation Draco can always be seen. The dragon looks down on Earth, watching it forever.

Dragons and snakes are also symbols of war. The hero of an ancient Greek poem has a serpent on his shield. The hero Hercules fought the dragon Ladon. Other stories say he tricked the dragon. Afterward, he placed an image of the dragon on his shield. One of the most-told stories about Draco involves Hercules.

▲ Depictions of dragons are ancient. This dragon guarded a gate to the ancient city of Babylon.

▶ Opposite page: This drawing from the 1700s shows Hercules fighting Ladon.

CHAPTER 3

The Story of Draco

Hercules was the son of Zeus, the king of the gods. Hercules's mother was a human princess named Alcmena. Zeus's wife, the goddess Hera, was jealous of Alcmena. Hera tried to kill her son, Hercules. But he grew strong and became a mighty man.

Later, jealous Hera caused Hercules to go mad. In a fit, he killed several people. Hercules felt horrible about what he had done. The gods said he had to go to his cousin Eurystheus to receive forgiveness. Eurystheus would give Hercules a set of difficult tasks. And if he could complete the tasks, he would become a god.

These labors were not easy. Hercules would have to be smart and brave. He fought a strong lion with his bare hands. He battled a monster with many heads. He chased down a swift and beautiful stag.

Finally Hercules had finished ten challenging labors. Next, he had to bring back three golden apples from the Garden of the Hesperides. The garden was located far away at the end of the world. Worse, it was guarded by the fierce dragon Ladon.

Ladon had one hundred heads. Born from the monsters Typhon and Echidna, the dragon was immortal. It could also change its voice. The titan Atlas also lived in the garden. Atlas held the sky on his shoulders. The dragon would allow only Atlas to come into the garden. Anyone else would have to fight Ladon.

TITANS
Titans are a major part of Greek mythology. The first titans, Gaia and Uranus, gave birth to more titans. These titans represented parts of nature such as the Sun. One titan, Zeus, started a war. His siblings Hades, Hestia, Demeter, Hera, and Poseidon helped him. They fought against the rest of the titans, who were led by Atlas. After battling for ten years, Zeus and his siblings were victorious. They became the Greek gods and lived on Mount Olympus. Most of the titans were imprisoned. Atlas was punished by having to hold the sky on his shoulders.

Hercules traveled through many lands and seas. Finally, he arrived at the garden. He knew Atlas could help him reach the golden apples. Hercules knew Ladon would allow Atlas to enter the garden. So he offered to hold the sky on his own shoulders.

This freed Atlas to safely pick the apples from the tree. Then Atlas and Hercules would switch places again. Hercules could take the apples back to Eurystheus and complete his task.

But Atlas was tired of holding up the sky. He decided to trick Hercules into taking his place. Atlas went past the dragon, entered the garden, and retrieved the apples. Meanwhile, Hercules bore the weight of the sky on his shoulders. But Atlas did not give the apples to Hercules. He wanted to leave Hercules holding up the sky. But Hercules figured out the trick. He told Atlas he needed to get a pad to protect his head and shoulders. So Atlas agreed to hold up the sky until Hercules came back. But Hercules left, taking the apples back to Eurystheus.

The goddess Hera was outraged that Hercules took the apples. The apples had been a wedding gift when she married Zeus. Hercules taking them was a double insult. Hera wanted to punish the dragon Ladon for losing the golden apples. She flung him into the sky.

As for Hercules, he became a god at the end of his life. The constellation Hercules is near Draco in the night sky. The dragon there has been beaten by the hero. Hercules's heel is crushing Draco's head.

CHAPTER 4

Draco in Other Cultures

Not all people who looked upon Draco saw a dragon. Some saw a snake or a hippopotamus. Some groups from the Middle East saw a dancer, camels, or a lute player. People in India saw an alligator. Israelites saw a case with arrows.

Stories of Draco as a snake or serpent are common. For many ancient cultures, a snake represented evil, confusion, and darkness. In Jewish and Christian teaching, the devil took the form of

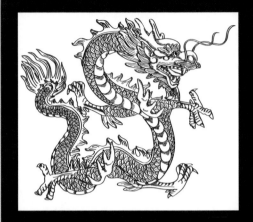

▲ Chinese dragons stand for wisdom and luck.

▶ Opposite page: A snake tempted Adam and Eve to take an apple in the Garden of Eden.

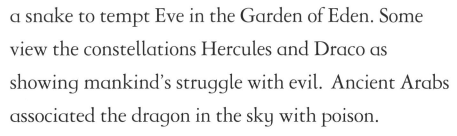

AN ANCIENT DRAGON

Some scholars believe the Old Testament of the Bible references Draco. The mention of Draco could date back to 1600 BC.

a snake to tempt Eve in the Garden of Eden. Some view the constellations Hercules and Draco as showing mankind's struggle with evil. Ancient Arabs associated the dragon in the sky with poison.

Yet other cultures view serpents as symbols of life or renewal. A Chinese myth involves two creatures that are half human and half snake. The creatures created order in the universe.

CHAPTER 5

How to Find Draco

Draco lies near the North Star. In the Northern **Hemisphere**, look for Draco in the summer. Late in the season, the dragon's eyes are nearly overhead.

Use the Big Dipper and the Little Dipper to find Draco. The middle of Draco's tail is right between them. To find Draco's head, look for the bright star Vega. It is part of the constellation Lyra. Trace the tail around the Little Dipper toward Vega to see Draco's body and head. The rest of the coiling dragon's tail twists around the Little Dipper.

▶ Opposite page: *Look for Draco near the Little Dipper.*

Glossary

asterism (AS-tuh-rih-zem)
An asterism is a well-known group of stars that is smaller than a constellation. Draco's head is an asterism of four stars.

astronomy (uh-STRAW-nuh-mee)
Astronomy is the study of stars and other objects in space. Astronomy is one of the oldest sciences.

axis (AK-sis)
An axis is an invisible line than runs through Earth from top to bottom. Earth rotates on its axis, which is slightly tilted.

galaxy (GAL-ax-ee)
A group of millions or billions of stars form a galaxy. Draco is home to the Spindle Galaxy.

gravity (GRAV-uh-tee)
Gravity is a force that pulls objects toward each other. Gravity holds each galaxy together.

hemisphere (HEM-uh-spheer)
One half of a planet is one hemisphere. You can see Draco from the Northern Hemisphere.

Mesopotamia (meh-sah-poh-TAY-mee-ah)
The area of ancient Mesopotamia is now Iraq, Syria, and Turkey. The Mesopotamians studied the stars.

mythology (mith-AH-luh-jee)
Mythology is a culture's set of stories or beliefs. Dragons appear many times in Greek mythology.

nebula (NEB-you-la)
A nebula is a cloud of gas and dust in space. Using a telescope, the scientist could see the nebula.

North Star (NORTH STAR)
The North Star is the star that shines directly above the North Pole and appears never to move in the sky. Draco is near the North Star.

polestar (POHL-star)
Polestar is another name for the North Star. One of the stars in Draco used to be Earth's polestar.

universe (YOU-nih-verse)
The universe is everything that exists in space. The universe could be made of billions or trillions of galaxies.

Learn More

Books

Driscoll, Michael. *A Child's Introduction to the Night Sky: The Story of the Stars, Planets, and Constellations—and How You Can Find Them in the Sky*. New York: Black Dog & Leventhal Publishers, 2004.

Mitton, Jacqueline. *Zoo in the Sky: A Book of Animal Constellations*. Washington, DC: National Geographic Society, 2006.

Rey, H. A. *Find the Constellations*. 2nd ed. Boston: Houghton Mifflin Harcourt, 2008.

Web Sites

Visit our Web site for links about Draco:

childsworld.com/links

Note to Parents, Teachers, and Librarians:
We routinely verify our Web links to make sure they are safe and active sites. So encourage your readers to check them out!

Index